PLAYING POKER WITH NANA

# Playing Poker
## with *Nana*

♣　♦　♥　♠

Megan McKenna

**VERITAS**

Published 2008 by
Veritas Publications
7/8 Lower Abbey Street
Dublin 1
Ireland

Email publications@veritas.ie
Website www.veritas.ie

ISBN 978-1-84730-120-8

Copyright © Megan McKenna, 2008

10 9 8 7 6 5 4 3 2 1

A catalogue record for this book is available from the British Library.

Designed by Lir Mac Cárthaigh
Set in 11pt Apollo MT with LTC Cloister Display
Printed in Ireland by ColourBooks Ltd.

Veritas books are printed on paper made from the wood pulp of managed forests. For every tree felled, at least one tree is planted, thereby renewing natural resources.

# Contents

♣ ♦ ♥ ♠

| | | |
|---|---|---|
| | Author's Note | 7 |
| | Introduction | 9 |
| 1. | Playing Poker with Nana | 12 |
| 2. | Two Pictures | 16 |
| 3. | The Good Old Days | 20 |
| 4. | The Statues from China | 26 |
| 5. | Rockaway Beach | 29 |
| 6. | Cuba 1960 | 33 |
| 7. | The Other Side of Her Door | 37 |
| 8. | Geraniums | 41 |
| 9. | The Jester's Prayer | 45 |
| 10. | History | 49 |
| 11. | All Souls' Day, November 2 | 51 |
| 12. | The Pickle Barrel, Pickle Puckering | 53 |
| 13. | No Accounting for Taste in the Human Race | 55 |
| 14. | On Loving | 57 |
| 15. | Nana's Prayer Book | 61 |
| 16. | Brownies – Comfort Food | 64 |
| 17. | Comfort Food – War Cake | 68 |
| | Afterword | 72 |

*With thanks to Chris Witt, dear friend, who gave me the idea for this book so long ago, when he told me a story about his grandmother and playing poker.*

*We must tell our stories to one another. They are our ties to the past and our lifelines for a future.*

# Author's Note

♣ ♦ ♥ ♠

WHEN I WRITE A BOOK — IT'S A GIFT, A give-away (like the Native peoples do after a person has died, in their memory) and once the words, the memories, the experiences, insights, descriptions are down on paper, they somehow become a gift for others and cease to be my sole property. I don't so much forget them as know them in a more solid fashion, making them tangible for others. They take on more substance, even, a life of their own, becoming something other than what they were when they were just my memories, intimations and experiences. The stories, when worded, are bridges, roads and the trajectories that memory, experience and knowledge travel towards others.

When I write I'm trying to do what I sometimes catch in a photograph — a tree reflected perfectly upside down in water, air exposed to light — a double image. I hope that's what people will see — through my words, my renderings, a glimpse of what was and is now reflected out towards others. Is it credible, verifiable, a true rendering? — it comes filtered through times (in this case more than sixty years-worth), distance, so many miles travelled from NYC, continents traversed. Is it true — oh, yes! It is a language born of place and relation, of memory and intensity, belief and practice besides words, collected stories and geographies.

[7]

I speak of photographs in this book. I have so few of my relatives: grandparents, aunts, uncles, all dead now. I am the oldest at sixty-one in an ancient matriarchy. The previous matriarch, my aunt Jane, died two years ago at ninety-five and I have metamorphosed into the head of a clan, the oldest woman of my tribe. It is sobering, surprising. I don't really sense it yet, though it's dawning on me more each day. The present is momentous, the past (just my sixty-four years carried within) I tell in stories of past moments – in this book captured in a sepia photograph or an object – and there are others not mentioned in this book – a doll with a china head, feet and hands, a lace doily, marrow bones on dark bread, a pair of silver scissors, a small hand mirror. What was once private is made public, yet private again – given to strangers in a kind of intimacy dared because of the depth of meaning I have found in them. Someone might really need what I have found or been given and it might really make a difference somewhere – it might just tip one person, a piece of the earth so that their lives and the world leans into an arc of wholeness. And so I tell the story. With Aunt Jane's death all the long strings have been severed to my family's immediate ancestry. They all dwell now in the unknown Mystery and it is we that forge the future and create a place worth dwelling within here for our grandchildren and those who come after us, down to the seventh generation. And so I pass on Nana to others – she was one of my best gifts ever.

MEGAN McKENNA

# *Introduction*

♣  ♦  ♥  ♠

THESE WORDS, STORIES, ENCAPSULATED BITS AND pearls of wisdom matter and give meaning. My Nana gave me a stubborn, relentless belief in living and an insistence that life, no matter how it twists and turns, is ultimately, even elegantly, *good*. To life she brought clarity, laughter, twinkling eyes, insights, glittering hopes that shimmer, insisting that a little glitz and glory goes a long way into every corner and crevice of ordinary life. A visit with Nana! Every summer it was two weeks to remember, mull over, reflect on, and look forward to the following year. It was always summer, and a trip to New York (I was born there but we'd moved away, my Dad being in the Navy). It was always like going home, July and August in Brooklyn, then Far Rockaway, then Flushing and Fresh Meadows, Queens with the Worlds' Fair grounds nearby and another world altogether for the duration of the visit.

She told me, though never actually in words, to be *fierce* and demanding, taking and giving to life all the passion and grace I could muster – whether I was nine, twelve, twenty-five, or now sixty. She saw through to essences. She lived through two world wars, then Korea, then Vietnam. She endured those times and said it perverts, maims and distorts *all* life, tears reality apart; children die before their parents which should never happen for any reason, and husbands and wives are separate – forcibly divided. Her husband died early.

I never knew my grandfathers and only knew my father's mother, Nana. They were both born on the same day and even that was important, even magical. How did she do that? Like so many other things she did in the usual course of just living.

We didn't talk about stuff much at home but, here, for two or three weeks, you could ask anything. She always answered with authority, sometimes looking stern in her flowered dress, aprons, sensible shoes, bun and granny glasses. It was a surety, as though she was both imparting knowledge and talking to me as an equal (not as an adult so much), but as someone of worth, deserving an answer, honestly. Being treated this way opened doors: to think, to wonder, to question, to disagree, to play with words, ideas, and fantasise. And it often began and returned again to the question: who was this woman? Or who were these women that lived inside of Nana? It was like those dolls that are nested one inside the other, tiny ones, small ones, always getting larger and larger, holding more and more inside them. There was drawing, tracing pictures, writing – it all started there. It was when and where I knew – discovered for the first time – that people had souls, that I had one! It was an essence of being, of singularity, but I didn't have words for it yet – I wouldn't for years.

This book is a gratitude and a witness to her courage, her faith and life and I only knew swatches of it, a bit here and there, being too self-absorbed until after she died at eighty-six and I was maybe twenty-five or twenty-six. There was a sixty-year difference. But I am sixty-four now and bridges are appearing. They are now visible though they were always there. I just didn't see a lot, or seeing, didn't know where the bridge went – though some I did step upon – and they brought me here, patterned my life, teased me and told me anything was possible, that life was limited only by my courage and faith.

It's amazing how often (and more as I get older) that her voice returns to me, and I hear her saying one-liners, or see her in my head – blue eyes dancing, looking at me over her wire-rimmed glasses – as though to say – What? Do you really believe that? Why are you doing that now? – and laughing at me without any sound, loudly and lovingly. This is the woman who would say to us so kindly: 'God never takes his eye off of you. He watches you every single moment but that's because he loves you so much! Just like I do.' And being loved by Nana was grand. I'd have to check out this God who seemed to accompany her all the time, like an invisible friend that I couldn't see yet. I was intrigued early though, maybe when I was six or seven years old.

— I —

# Playing Poker with Nana

♣  ♦  ♥  ♠

THERE WERE A LOT OF US, SO WE WERE FARMED
out, usually three at a time for a couple of weeks
every summer to New York. We made the rounds of
the relatives. My mother and father didn't have a
lot of family: my mother's eldest brother married my father's
eldest sister. My parents met at my aunt and uncle's engage-
ment party. There were stories of my father chasing my
mother around the basement (he was a long-distance runner).
He ran cross country for the US in the Olympics in the early
1930s and there were pictures and stories of their courting,
with my mother standing in all kinds of weather as my father
ran by – the marathon later replaced cross country. Years after
he won a gold medal (the group after those portrayed in
*Chariots of Fire,* the movie) that became my mother's wedding
ring. There were jokes that the marriage would last as long as
the record held – it lasted nearly fifty-seven+ years.

We'd plan on going to Nana's all year long. We'd save our
money to play poker with her. And we'd come home about
10–15 pounds heavier from each trip. My mother was always
asking us what we did to put on the weight? Basically we *ate*
lots. Dinner was a major event – meat, potatoes, peas piled
high and gravy. It was delicious but we each started out with
a heaping plate and Nana was ever ready, spoon in hand, for
seconds. We knew there was dessert coming too, apple pie, ice
cream, peach cobbler – and we tried to pace ourselves. If you

refused she'd look pained and say softly: 'You don't love me.' The first time she said it, it shocked. Afterwards I learned what food meant to Nana. Besides the pounds it put on, food was security, hope for a future. She'd come over to the US in the hold of a ship, eating moldy bread and rotting potatoes. For her, food was life, 'making it', meant to be shared in thanksgiving. An excess of food was the ability to feed others, a tangible sign of being able to share wealth. This was the heritage of a generation or more of immigrants who had been hungry for so long, coming to America, the land of plenty. Food was for gathering and being thankful, utterly grateful for life – in a word, food was love given. So we smiled, and ate slowly.

After dinner there were two options – the choice decreed by the Brooklyn Dodgers baseball schedule. She was more than an avid fan – for her they were family. She knew everything about them. Batting averages, scores, runs brought in, who was traded from where, for whom, home boys, slumps and their personal lives – marriages, births, children, divorces (shame on them!), salaries, height, weight, ages and religions. And she gave a running commentary so we'd know all the crucial background information. And she prayed for them – not so much that they'd win. She said that was in the hands of God and how well they played – the hands/gloves of the pitcher, catcher, outfielders and their eye on the ball. But concentration – that was affected by their personal lives – it had to be. So she prayed they'd clean up their acts, fly right and have a winning season.

No game – ah, that's what we had saved for all year. Quarters, nickels and dimes (no pennies, too heavy to carry). We usually came with about 25–40 bucks each – a lot to accumulate in the fifties when you're only nine or ten years old. And poker was serious business. Night after night at the dining room table – no one would even think of doing something else or missing the game. Even stick ball games were relegated to late after-noons before dinner.

And two to three weeks later we'd go home, fatter and richer. I remember the year my mother found out. Somebody left their stash out and Mom wanted to know where we'd gotten that kind of money. There was a lot of hemming and hawing but it leaked out – playing poker with Nana! For money! My mom was aghast and went yelling after my father: 'Frank! Frank! Did you know about this?' If he did, he wasn't saying anything – a wise and often quiet man. 'She's *your* mother – you have to talk to her.' I could tell by the look on his face – he had no intention of saying anything. He knew better than that – she was his mother!

It was only years later when I was maybe twenty-four or twenty-five that I began to wonder about those poker games, or more to the point, all the money we went home with – double and sometimes triple the amount we came with to Nana's place – nearly $100 or more! I decided I had to know: did she cheat and let us win? In an Irish family that was a mortal sin!

So I invited myself to dinner. Same house, same table, even same dinner: roast beef, mashed potatoes, peas with onions, lots of gravy and afterwards apple pie. As per the ritual, the table was cleared and the cards came out, but the stakes had gone up substantially from a quarter or fifty cents a hand, and max a dollar. We started at twenty dollars a hand and I promptly started losing! Twenty to sixty dollars gone and the night was still young. I thought it best to take a breather and ask the questions that had been bothering me for months. 'Nana do you remember when we would come, as kids during the summer to stay with you?' 'Sure,' she said. 'We'd play poker.' 'Sure,' she said again. 'Well, I've been thinking about that.' This time she looked up – 'Yes' – leading me on. And I blurted it out. 'We'd save our money all year – allowances, gifts, extra work and we'd play practically every night. Some nights we'd lose, some we'd win. Some nights we'd win big and others we'd lose miserably, a couple of bucks or big stashes.' I paused. She didn't say anything. 'Well,' I went on, 'I was thinking lately that even though we'd lose and win and lose, we *always* went home with a lot of money – like double what we brought with us to New York – sometimes even $100!' I hesitated. 'Yes?' she was still leading me on. 'Well I was wondering. Did you cheat? Did you let us win?' Her eyebrows went up. There was a pause. She took off her glasses. This was serious and she looked at me.

I was taken aback – she didn't answer me, instead she had a question or two of her own to ask. 'You're going to that seminary school aren't you?' (I was studying for a masters' degree in theology.) 'Yes,' I said. 'Well what are you studying there?' 'Theology,' I said. 'What's that?' 'Un … the study of God.' Even as I said it, it did sound rather preposterous. She laughed out loud. 'You know,' she said, 'for someone as smart and sharp as you are, sometimes you're really slow and dumb.' I was shocked now! 'What do you mean?' Her answer came hard and fast. 'You said it yourself – when you play poker with your Nana, sometimes you win a little. Sometimes you lose, even lose a lot, but if you haven't learned by now that you can't really ever lose playing poker with your Nana – how will you ever learn that when you play with God you never ever really lose!' I was stunned.

'Oh, you'll win some. You'll lose – lots at times, even everything it will seem, but if you really play and it's high stakes, with God – you'll never *ever* lose!' And she smiled, her blue eyes twinkling and put her wire-rimmed glasses back on and dealt the next hand. First lesson, words of wisdom: you never ever lose with God – no matter what!

# Two Pictures

♣  ♦  ♥  ♠

### The Girl with the Watering Can

My Grandmother's apartment in the brownstone walk-up was small. I didn't realise this until I went back in my twenties. The few rooms, the worn carpets, and the two pictures were still there. The first in the living room over a bookcase stuffed with books and treasures including two Chinese figurines, delicately hand-painted. I have them now (but that's another story). This first picture was an inexpensive print from the Met (Metropolitan Museum of Art) but I didn't know that then. It seemed to be in a place of honour and I assumed for years that it was of my grandmother when she was a little girl, my age, maybe seven or eight, almost nine.

The girl in the picture stood alone, as far as I could tell, in a huge sprawling garden – the flowers, many of them, from my vantage point looking up, seemed to stand taller, higher than she did. I was fascinated by her clothes, especially her shoes: they were high, black and buttoned up. They seemed to plant her there, sturdy. She fit in with that garden – as if growing along with all those wild flowers and weeds. All around her seemed a delicate world. She had a dress and a pinafore or apron over her dress, or a coat with the dress sticking out below her knees. Her lace pantaloons showed beneath her dress that was edged in lace up the front, buttoned to her neck and at the cuffs, and what appeared to be a bow in the back. She was blonde; hair framing her face, with bangs and long to her shoulders with pink cheeks, demure yet somehow ruddy and healthy.

And she held a watering can, just like the one Nana used to water all the plants in her apartment. I wondered if she'd brought it over with her or found one like it here. I'd ask to water the plants, just to use the watering can. It was heavy to me and yet in the picture the little girl didn't seem to find it heavy at all. It was part of her, like an extension of her hand. I wanted to be like her — like Nana, of course.

However, in my teens I saw that print — actually the painting itself — and found out it was Auguste Renoir's 'The Girl With the Watering Can'. How could that be? How could I actually have thought for so long that it was Nana? I was mortified.

**The Second Picture**
The other picture was a photograph, eight by ten inches in a wrought iron frame, which sat on top of her bureau, on a hand crocheted lace doily which she had made herself. It was a young woman, not yet twenty, dressed elegantly with a bustle in the back, her hair piled up high and a hat perched on top of her head — a proper bonnet I was told. She had reddish brown hair, her head tilted as though she was looking right at me, probing, asking her own questions. My grandmother had been an adventurer — she had crossed the ocean when she was thirteen or fourteen — I wouldn't do it for another two decades until I was nearly thirty-five. She looked so sure of herself, self-contained, pretty but not 'sweet', more gutsy. She could have been a heroine in the movies, I was sure of that! I'd looked at her and loved the idea that I looked like her.

But it wasn't her! It was her mother, my great grandmother back in Ireland. She had the same name though, Alice Veronica. There had been a number of them (my sister is named after her and my middle name is Alice). I fancied that I resembled my grandmother — I had been told that, but I had raven hair, no red tresses. And she was now a woman in her sixties, grey hair pulled into a bun at the base of her neck. She wore sensible shoes, worn and faded dresses and I wondered what must have happened in those intervening years. How did she turn from the girl in the garden into the young woman with the red hair and flashing eyes, long dress and riding outfit to the grandmother of the flowered housecoats. (I seemed to omit the part in her life for years where she was my father's mother and had given birth to at least four – I later learned more – children and had been wife and mother.) But there were so few pictures in the house – these were all I had to work with, and my fertile imagination.

And these two pictures – though neither of them were actually she! Such massive miscalculation! Assumptions utterly without basis.

In the late sixties I had been in a convent – the old fashioned kind – wearing those high laced-up shoes (like boots) and a long black dress with stiffly starched white collar and cuffs that were changed weekly. When I left I was distressed and a bit lost for a while. During this time, I was sitting in her living room one day and she gave me sage advice when she saw me looking at the girl with the watering can. She laughed, took a twenty out of her weathered coin purse and said: 'Honey, go get yourself some decent and comfortable shoes, with some colour in them – not like those in the picture – to take you back into life.' That's when I told her about my impressions of the pictures, that I was sure they were her and that I had wanted to be like her – then and now. I told her that I'd look at the pictures and think I was looking at myself caught in another face and time. Seems I had been about myself and others for a long time and just didn't realise how much.

Then she announced seriously: 'Position in life is everything!' And I thought, what has *that* got to do with anything? My confusion must have shown. She explained: 'Both of those pictures were displayed in places of honour over the curio cabinet with all my saved treasures and in the bedroom on the bureau where I put my watch and ring, so, of course you would think they were special and important and that they were precious to me. And to your child's eye, *of course,* they were me.' She smiled. I got the feeling she liked the idea of her being mistaken for the girl with the watering can, and for her mother, left behind in Ireland so many decades ago. She went on, 'Position in life *is* everything. Don't you forget that. You looked up, saw them and wanted to *be* them. The world looks so different from below – more so than it does from above, looking down on others. Always look up to people and you'll see an inner truth about who they really are inside – what you'd never be able to see if you look down on them. Being below and being down, close to the ground isn't a bad place to be. It's being humble, meaning close to the ground *(humus)*.' She'd studied Latin as a girl in Catholic school and remembered such things. 'That means you know who you are – no matter what others think of you. You know yourself truly – the good and the not so good.'

'You *are* the girl with the watering can and have something of your great grandmother, Mary Murray, because you wanted to be like them. Be careful who you look up to – you will become like them. You could do a lot worse than Renoir's little girl or your great grandmother at twenty. And remember, who knows who's been watching you and looking up at you, maybe for a long time already! Position in life *is* everything.'

# — 3 —

# *The Good Old Days*

♣ ♦ ♥ ♠

*Auld Lang Syne'*
*The year is going let him go;*
*ring out the false, ring in the true*
 — Alfred Lord Tennyson

'Old long ago, or times long past' is the ancient meaning of the words to that poem and song that is often sung at the end of each year. There are memories, pieced together of a place inside, but no recollections of the street: 84th and 3rd Avenue, or the outside, or impressions of the neighbourhood, except for the stoop — the steps in front of the brownstone of my Nana's house. The 'biddies', as many called them, would sit on the stoop, or on the front steps just below the entrance way, and talk, gossip away most of the late afternoons. We usually gave them a wide berth. We were intent on more important things than words and accounts of whom in the parish had done what or who in the neighbourhood was up to no good again. Especially if it was high summer and so hot you could fry an egg on the sidewalk (we'd tried it and it did fry! It stuck to the concrete like crazy glue). We were intent on opening the fire hydrant and letting loose pillars and sprays of water — or 'up to no good' as they'd frown and say, shaking their heads at us and murmuring (loud enough for us to catch) things like … oh, in my day, when we were growing up, we'd never do anything like that! We wouldn't be allowed to! Nowadays, though, they let them get away with murder – shameful, awful, what will become of them – and on and on and on they went.

The hydrant wouldn't stay open for long, maybe ten or fifteen minutes, just enough time to soak down, run around barefoot, screaming our heads off, oblivious to the heat for a short while, playing in streams of water shooting out like a cannon. Then with the help of a garbage can lid redirect the water straight up and out in a shower for as long as two or three kids could get it close to the source – then, exhausted, they'd drop it and it would come out streaming hard and icy cold again – punctuated by more squeals, yells and pushing and running around.

The cops would come and stand there disapprovingly but allow it to remain open for another couple of minutes. Then they'd make a show of getting down off their horses, or clearing the way and getting behind the hydrant before they actually turned it off. They knew how long it would be before the water pressure in businesses and homes would be affected. They also knew that most of the kids and gangs in the neighbourhood would now be more subdued after all the shouting and getting soaked; we'd calm down and the heat wouldn't seem so bad. It was usually the ten to twelve year-olds who actually opened the hydrant but, after that, it was anybody's game. Even the older boys and girls would get in on it. It made your day, especially when it was stifling inside, even with all the windows and doors opened, and not a breeze anywhere. Sweating, even if you barely moved or hardly breathed. Afterwards, we'd hang around in our wet soggy shorts and tops, clothes sticking to us, hair drenched, and find a spot in the shade of the stoop or an overhang and rest.

And we'd notice that the group of ladies would be 'tsking' and fretting again (years later I heard it called 'whinging and whining' by the Irish on the Aran Islands off the west coast there, and it suited them aptly). It was all the talk of the 'good old days', times past, the way things were rememered in glowing terms, idyllic, carefree, when everyone seemed to obey – in fact did what they were told without even being asked! It seemed then there was no violence, no crime, great rapport with neighbours and all the younger ones, whatever their ages, were duly respectful of their elders and knew they were to be seen and not heard (mostly).

Later upstairs, setting the table for supper, we'd mimic them. And once we were caught by Nana who frowned. We stopped immediately but she got very, very serious, thoughtful, and wiped her hands on her apron. And when she turned to us it was in a very firm voice: 'Don't you listen to those old biddies. They don't know what they're talking about. They've gotten mean in their old age [same age as her!]. They haven't learned a thing, constantly harping back to a past that never was. They're stringing pipe dreams like unhappy children – except they should know better.' Nana was going at it – which she did so rarely that we'd stopped everything and paid close attention to what she was saying. And she knew what she was talking about. It was time to listen up, when she spoke in that tone of voice, with such force and surety.

'The good old days – damn 'em!' she said. 'No such thing, ever! You know what those supposedly good old days were actually like? [*and* she didn't wait for a response from any of us.] I'll tell you what they were like' and a litany I'll never forget began to pour forth from her:

- ♣ It was mud in the streets inches deep, slop, garbage, dodging manure, horses, wagons and every contraption imaginable.
- ♦ It was five and six floor walk-ups and sometimes ten or more people to an apartment.
- ♥ It was soot, coal bins and old furnaces in the basement; and fires would break out in the tenements made mostly of wood and then they'd rip through, leaving families, sometimes three generations out in the cold with nothing.
- ♠ There was nearly no heat in winter, frigid cold and equally awful heat in summer and no relief.
- ♣ It was children as young as you are (we were between six and eleven) or even younger spending ten to twelve hours a day working at piece labour in factories.
- ♦ It was the constant threat of someone losing their job,

the dole and going without even more to make ends meet.

♥ It was being trapped in a couple of blocks in a neighbourhood and past that might as well have been another country – dangerous, no one you knew and often you didn't know their language.

♠ And war, always another war. [She looked away from us and stopped. We thought she'd finished, then she continued …]

♣ And worst of all cholera and influenza ran through a building and took one at least, and, all too often, two or three from a family, your little brother or sister, an aunt, a father, no one escaped, year, after year, after year.

She took a breath. All her words seemed to catch up with her and tears welled up in her eyes. 'You had aunts and uncles you never met, buried in a box when they were two or three, six, even just a couple of weeks old.' She waited a minute and regained her composure. Then she wrung her hands and rubbed them and said adamantly: 'That's what the good old days were like. It's good to see them go and I hope we'll never see them come again. Oh, there's plenty wrong with today, but it's not like the good old days. You'd never want to have lived them. Don't listen to anyone who keeps on about the good old days – the only truth you'll learn from them is that they don't much like living now and are unhappy with what they made of what was given them. And they, being miserable, don't take kindly to anyone else enjoying themselves or really living now. Be thankful that you didn't know the good old days. You've got these days now. They're the only ones you'll ever have. Live 'em. Use 'em. Make them better for those you love and those who come after you. Don't waste any part of your life pining for something that never was.'

'Those folks trying to live stuck back there in the "good old days" aren't facing reality, and are busy making others miserable. Bless today and all that's in it and make it all worthwhile.' Then, realising she'd talked more in the last ten minutes than she had in a week or more, she fiddled with the silverware, smiled (composed again) and said: 'You're doing a good job on the table. Come, get some ice water and I'll check on the roast and the potatoes.' And life — in these good old days — would pick up its pace again.

Nana knew that entire poem by Tennyson and she would recite it for us, in a sing-song voice towards the end of every year. She knew that to take a line or two out of context was to alter and distort the memory and the intent of the poem. And there are things that you must remember in their entirety:

IN MEMORIAM (EXTRACT)
Ring out, wild bells, to the wild sky,
The flying cloud, the frosty light:
The year is dying in the night:
Ring out, wild bells, and let him die.

Ring out the old, ring in the new,
Ring, happy bells, across the snow:
The year is going, let him go;
Ring out the false, ring in the true.
Ring out the grief that saps the mind,
For those that here we see no more;
Ring out the feud of rich and poor,
Ring in the redress to all mankind.

Ring out a slowly dying cause,
And ancient forms of party strife;
Ring in the nobler modes of life,
With sweeter manners, purer laws.

Ring out old shapes of foul disease:
Ring out the narrowing lust of gold;
Ring out the thousand wars of old,
Ring in the thousand years of peace.

Her vehemence and passion ambush me still. If there is no such thing as 'the good old days' then what will our children and our grandchildren remember us and our times for — this century past when the human race managed to kill more of its own kind, more of each other than in the history of the world to this point? And this century seems to be intent on continuing the killing exponentially. Will they look at one another and the earth we bequeathed to them and wonder: 'What were they thinking back in those days?'

Nana always repeated the last line of the poem, with emphasis, almost as a demand: 'Ring in the thousand years of peace.' I've added it to my years' end reflections and prayer, in her honour and memory.

— 4 —

# The Statues from China

♣  ♦  ♥  ♠

THERE WERE, IN THE LIVING ROOM, TWO PIECES of furniture that I found intriguing. One was a round mahogany table, scalloped around the edges, deep shining so that you could see yourself reflected in it, but with nothing on it, because it wasn't like most tables sitting firmly and roundly on a pedestal. This one was bent over and the top faced flat out. It was used for a number of occasions when it was placed upright like a normal table.

Sometimes it was a shrine (mostly in the month of May) with a statue of Mary placed on it, with rosary beads, and some paper flowers, all on a lace doily. And on rare occasions, a small real flower in a tiny bud vase was placed there. Or when there were lots of people over for dinner it was used for the desserts, tempting, smelling great and not to be touched until the big table had been cleared. And often, when I came to visit later, she'd place her reading glasses, a pitcher of water or tea cosy and cup, along with *The New York Times* crossword puzzle on this table. The Sunday crossword stayed on the table until it was finished, usually a couple of days; it would rarely take a whole a week. The daily crossword was done early in the morning when it arrived and quickly! She said, as I'd watch her: 'There are a lot of words you get to know, you'd only use them in crossword puzzles, "trivia" knowledge; can't ever imagine using them in a sentence – they're usually three- or four-letter words, like an antelope from Africa, remote geographical places, words for harems and Asian servants or exotic things. It's like anything else you do all the time, you get good at it, fast and easily … and you never know when a word will come in handy or a piece of information will be useful. And sometimes, just knowing all those places and things exist, remind you of just how big the world really is and that it's always out there waiting for you to find it, to pay a visit.'

The second piece of furniture was a lawyer's bookcase with glass doors that lifted up on each shelf and the ones towards the bottom had glass doors that opened out. Inside were treasures – not to be touched or played with, only looked at and studied. We weren't even allowed to dust there.

The pieces I remember most were two Chinese figures about eight or ten inches high. They were a man and a woman, oriental, far eastern and strange and beautiful. They were Chinese – a pair. There were also two Chinese vases in her apartment that had been made into lamps; they had been wedding presents. They went to my aunt, then to one of my sisters, passed on and cherished as they moved to Florida, then to Washington, DC and found new homes. I wondered how did these far away things come across oceans and land in Brooklyn, New York?

The figurines were hand painted, a lot of greens, glazed silver, ash, pale, subtle and muted tones, delicately executed. The woman with her fan stood turned slightly away from me. She seemed to flow, to move, to almost be dancing from her posture. A long dress, tiny feet, hair elaborately coiffed – every bit of her was perfect – a Chinese lady.

The other was a fisherman. They were together but did not 'go together'. He was of the same colours and hues, though a bit darker and shadowed and more spare in detail. He held a fishing pole instead of a fan, complete with line and a wriggling fish. I always wanted to hold them, touch them, see what they felt like though I'd been warned over and over that they were so fragile they might easily break. They had been a gift from my grandfather, who had died long before I was born (he'd been a fireman) and anything he'd given Nana was cherished and off limits to all of us grandchildren when we came to visit.

One night we'd gotten ready for bed and we had been cutting up, reluctant to let the day end and go to sleep. (Time always seemed to go so much faster at Nana's house than at home.) Pyjamas were on, teeth brushed, the bathroom was a mess from toothpaste squirts, lumps on the sink (maybe the floor too). I was standing alone looking at them, thinking they were like real people in China. Nana came over and opened the cabinet and lifted out one, then the other and stood them carefully on the round table, after putting a doily down for them to stand on. She said: 'You can hold one, but please be careful. I don't know what I'd do if one of them broke'. And I reached for one, the woman, quickly. She grabbed my wrist, 'Be careful,' again drawing out that word so I heard it, 'be full of care.'

This time I moved more slowly and picked it up gingerly with both hands. It was cold to the touch. 'Porcelain china, made in China' was written on the bottom side with more writing in Chinese characters. I held it, running my fingers over it reverently because it meant so much to her. We were silent. I sighed and put it down carefully and picked up the fisherman. I was awed by the details: the fish and its scales, minute ridges of his beard, the folds of his clothing. How long I held them, I have no idea. No word was said but the world stopped for a while; time shifted. I learned to look, *to see,* and probably took the first step in the art and discipline of contemplation (a long loving look at reality – that's half the definition, more to come later). Then I placed them back on the table and stepped back to see them together outside their shelf under glass. Then Nana put them back in their familiar places and lowered the glass door.

We were just there as it got darker outside and the shadows lengthened in the room. She said very quietly, just between the two of us, 'Now you know how you're supposed to live all the time. Don't squeeze life like it's a toothpaste tube. Finger it carefully like fine china', and with that she ran her hand across my cheek bones and down the ridge of my nose, 'and kiss it like goodnight'. And she kissed me on the forehead, turned me around and pointed me towards the bedroom.

I'm sure I dreamed of going to China that night. I did go, nearly forty-eight years later, and saw it with awe both through the eyes of a ten-year-old girl and my Nana's eyes at sixty.

— 5 —

# *Rockaway Beach*

♣ ◆ ♥ ♠

NANA HAD A BEACH HOUSE IN ROCKAWAY ON LONG Island. I don't remember practically anything about it except the linoleum in the kitchen where it wrinkled and curled up and the board-walk where I would spend hours, away from the glare of the sun, quietly watching the waves and the people walking above me and out on the beach, unaware their snatches of conversation were being studied and listened to from below. My dad would usually work in the city Monday through Friday and take the ferry out for the weekend. We all lined up at the end of the dock waiting for the ferry; it was the official start of the weekend for us, when dad came off the ferry, waving to us. We would wait for him to come to each of us, kissing and hugging us in turn, but not saying very much.

While we waited – the ferry was often late – there was free entertainment. A group of boys, around fifteen or sixteen I think, would take turns diving off the pier for the coins, pennies and nickels we'd pitch into the water. The water was deep enough for a ferry to dock and it took years of practice and skill for them to hold their breath. It always looked murky and dark but nowhere near as polluted as it would be years later, though the water had its share of junk and garbage – old tires, rocks, clothes, paper and cans. They'd dive in and straight down into that mysterious dark and seem to stay down there forever. We'd count, worry, and gasp when they'd surface, gulping for air. And if they'd gotten the coin, if they'd successfully angled their bodies for the plunge at the point where it hit the water, they'd hold it aloft triumphantly. We would cheer them on and another coin, sometimes even a quarter, would be tossed out further to test their endurance and courage.

Often they'd come up empty handed, take a long draft of air and go down again and again. Sometimes getting it, or more likely bringing up something else – a shoe, a trinket, or a plastic ball snagged on the bottom. Once in a while they'd come up grinning and shouting, having grabbed at something on the bottom as they shoved off, heading up to the light again – a watch that still worked or maybe a dollar coin. Once when I was there, a boy came up with a diamond bracelet. Then he shinned up the side of the pier – his game over for the evening, delighted with his unexpected 'catch'. I wanted to join them but made the mistake of saying so and was threatened within an inch of my young life if I should ever go near that pier unless dad was expected from the ferry. It would be another decade before I took any such plunges and risks!

The Saturday morning ritual with dad on the island was never missed. We'd be up at the crack of dawn (or before), dressed and waiting to go to the bakery. The shop was filled with things we couldn't imagine how to make, but loved to eat: cruellers, bear claws, napoleons, Danish – cheese, apple, prune, and berry, coffee cakes with crumble topping, and doughnuts, even jelly doughnuts. We were allowed to choose *one,* eat it as fast or as slowly as we wanted – to have the choice was indeed a treat, instead of us eating what we were served. We could gulp it down or drag it out for a half hour, just as we liked.

I always went for the jelly doughnuts. They were big, fat, thick, covered in powered sugar, and when you hit the jelly it was luscious and there was lots of it. I'd wondered how they got the jelly in there, before or after they baked it, and discovered soon enough, after diligent research before eating each one, the tiny opening indicating where the jelly was squished inside even though sometimes it was covered over with sugar.

Remedy for that problem: eat or lick all the sugar off slowly from the outside of the doughnut. Sometimes the tiny puncture had closed up and it wasn't visible any longer.

Saturday after Saturday would fly by (the summer was counted out in bakery visits and the number and quality of the jelly doughnuts, sometimes they were truly memorable and remarkable). And then it happened. An ordinary Saturday (if there was ever such a thing), jelly doughnut in hand, I decided to make it last as long as I could. I nibbled at the edges, ate all the sugar off, now sticky, and held with two fingers, one on the doughy inside. And I took itty-bitty bites, looking, anticipating when I would hit that sweet taste of jelly. I was half in and no jelly. One quarter left and no jelly. What was wrong? Well, you would think it was the end of the world. I ate the whole thing and there was no jelly! I'd been robbed! False advertisement. No jelly. I deserved another, immediately. I was loud and public in my disappointment.

Finally, later in the day, after hearing about this dang jelly doughnut minus jelly for hours on end, Nana marched me down the boardwalk. I knew I was in for it – I'd been a pain in the neck all day. Up to the edge of the pier we went, in stony silence. We stood there for a bit and she said: 'You know, I'm very disappointed in you.' Now *that* was the worst thing she could say to me. I was near to tears and choked up. She stood looking out over the deep water, no ferry in sight. She was very close to the edge. 'Come here,' she said, indicating that I should stand beside her, closer than I'd ever been to the edge of the pier. 'A couple of weeks ago,' she began, 'remember that boy who dove down after a nickel and came up empty handed and he dove again and again and finally he was just determined to find something, anything.' I nodded. 'Well,' she said, 'what did he find?' I remembered: 'a diamond bracelet!' 'Yes, and I bet he wasn't expecting that … was he?' 'No way,' I answered, wondering where this was going.

'Well,' she said, 'it could be the same thing with you and your jelly doughnut.' She'd lost me. 'Life is funny, you know. We get used to wanting things the same way … to doing the same thing over and over and expecting the same result time and again. Predictability. We take the same route to the beach, to church, to the bakery, the bus stop, the pier, instead of trying out a new way each time. Why, we even sit in the same pew in church and go to the same mass so we won't have to be too chummy with new people. You've got to learn that this is no way to live, no way to live at all. It makes life boring. Life should always be bigger than that, more mysterious than we'll ever know. Look down there. What can you see?'

'Not much,' I said. 'It's water, different colours.' I already knew the light penetrated to certain depths and so the water looked green, or grey or black and when the sun was really strong it danced across the water glinting and blinding. 'It's deep.' 'Yes,' she said, 'and who really knows what's underneath there, lost, hidden, waiting to be found after years and years. Sometimes it's never found.' I was intrigued. Her voice changed to that tone I later dubbed wise or intimate, like someone sharing a precious secret. 'You know, honey, God made this earth and left all sorts of things hidden in it and made it so that the things you think you know for sure don't always hold true. In fact, she said, it helps to know that, with God, you never get what you expect and you always get more than what you bargained for!'

'Now, you go back to the beach and be quiet for a while and think about that jelly doughnut and no jelly. What could you have learned? What did you get instead of the jelly? Remember: you never get what you expect and you always get MORE than what you bargained for.' And that was thrown out and left all sorts of things. I was hooked and caught in the mystery of life, ever more deeply, as the years went by – and I still once in a while get a jelly doughnut just to see if there's jelly in it or what else might be hidden in its absence – it's lingering absence and lack.

— 6 —

# Cuba 1960

♣  ♦  ♥  ♠

'Sweetie, don't you dare despair. You're not allowed to.' I was fifteen, young and naïve, living near Washington, DC and the world barged in during the Cuban missile crisis. It dominated the news, the tension was palpable and it grew thicker by the hour. They'd interrupt classes at school and tell us to pray that we wouldn't go to war or the missiles wouldn't be fired, that Cuba would stand down. But they'd repeat again and again that the United States was not going to be the country that would relent, we were going to call their bluff.

I can remember the first taste of outright, cold-blooded fear. This was the dawning reality of evil, of death, intended, imminent, planned and executed, of war intruding on my life of a half-dozen friends, class schedules, playing basketball, my family and the latest music or dance craze. Suddenly nothing fit. The universe had shifted and it was all 'off', out of focus. Everything, in fact, was in jeopardy: my life (I was selfishly thinking of the two or three dozen people I knew and cared about). It could be over before it got going at all.

I went to bed upstairs in the room I shared with two other sisters, one older and one younger. I curled up and couldn't even cry. I was shaking in terror. Conjuring up TV newsreels over and over again of aerial photographs, missile silos, President Kennedy's words; pictures of an angry, bearded Fidel Castro and thousands of faces behind him shouting. I knew little of missiles except from footage of scenes from Hiroshima and Nagasaki in 1945, the year after I was born. And just watching them did something in the pit of my stomach, making me sick – the flash point and spreading ominous cloud of blackness engulfing everything – then black and white pictures of dazed children, half naked, their clothes hanging off in pieces with their skin shredded, screaming and running, or wandering around lost. I couldn't absorb it all and I just shut down. I turned my face to the wall. I was learning not only fear and how it can paralyse you but anger at the world, at the human race – vaguely and generally – and at leaders who did not consider real individual people in their war plans and posturing politics. I was learning despair.

It was one of the few times I remember that Nana had come to visit us and was staying for a couple of weeks. When I refused to come down she had to climb the stairs to me. I was refusing food, lunch and dinner, and refusing to talk to anyone. I was trapped in my own world and it was narrow and tight and no one was going to get in.

She stood by the bed for a long time. I knew she was there. I heard her slow progress up each step, holding onto the banister. I didn't turn over … She didn't say anything for the longest time and when she did I couldn't believe how much anger and rage there was in her voice, but love too, unmistakably love. 'Don't you dare despair. It's not allowed. Ever. Don't you dare, you hear me? Sweetie, don't do it. Don't let them kill your spirit.' I don't know how many times she said the words. Maybe it was just once, or a couple of times. Even now I think of them over and over, like a mantra seeded deep inside me.

I turned over and made room for her on the bed (a single bed so it was tight, me against the wall and her ample girth filling up the rest of the space). 'I'm afraid,' I said. 'I know,' she said, 'and that's good. You've got good reason to be afraid. At least you know that much. It's a place to start. The world can be an awful place. There's wrong, evil, sin, violence, injustice, killing, war – practically all of it unnecessary but done by otherwise decent people in the name of one thing or another: nations and states, saving the world from something like communism or facism, the barbarians – there are always the others, the evil ones, Satan, the devil incarnate and we're always the good ones even if we saved the world – or that part of it – by killing them all and bombing their homes, and destroying everything that was life. Both sides. Always saying the same thing – that God, it seems, is on *our* side, *their* side, both sides. And you must learn very quickly that God is not on the side of anyone who kills, no matter what anyone says. We do that sort of thing all by ourselves.'

'I've seen so much war. Everywhere it seems to break out, all the time. You get over one and they can't seem to last long without setting it up and looking for an opportunity to start another one. I grew up listening to stories of war and killing, then the First World War, "the war to end all wars", and the victors were ruthless, setting up the Second World War, then the Korean war, the Cold war, now this in Cuba [the Vietnam war was yet to come]. It would be my generation's war and more than half, sometimes three quarters of my graduating class would kill or be killed halfway around the world, in a country we had to find on maps, that was suddenly a threat to life everywhere, and here in the US.'

'Now sit up,' she said. 'This is crucial. Now you know what it means to grow up fast, overnight' – childhood was instantly ripped away and gone forever that day – 'But you have to know your part in all this and how you're involved.' I was listening hard and trying to understand.

'First, what's wrong with the world is wrong with you.' She let that one sink in for a while. 'But,' she went on, 'that also means that what's right with the world is right with you too. We're all human beings and anything anyone else can do, no matter how horrible, insane or impossibly evil and sick, you're just as capable of doing. We all hurt each other in the same ways. We all bleed and scream and are afraid of the same things. There are people all over this country and in Cuba and everywhere else shaking and frightened just like you.'

'Sweetie, do you believe in God?' 'Of course I do,' I said. 'Well, if you do, you can't despair. You're not allowed to. God made us all – all the same. Eyes, ears, hearts and hopes, aches and pains, fears and hate and loves. And we're all made in God's image – *this* is what those words in the Bible mean.

What's wrong with the world is wrong with you. And what's right with the world is right with you. We're all in this together. You can't turn your face to the wall and stop feeling and talking. You can't – you're not allowed. God didn't make us to kill, or to give up on each other, to give up on anyone he made, or the earth he made. If you believe – you're not allowed to despair. Now get up, go wash your face and comb your hair and come downstairs.'

With her arm around me we went downstairs. I don't remember dinner or after, or much else. I got over the fear, at least the shakes, though it returns all too often because of the world and what we do to each other – but I cannot totally blame anyone for what others do, without looking hard into myself, my generation, my country, my religion and saying, as though in confession and acknowledgement, her words of truth-telling. 'What's wrong with the world is wrong with you, with us – but what's right with the world is right with us – all of us (including "them" whoever they happen to be this time). And that always opens a door, and with the fresh air that comes in, despair must exit.'

A week after she went back to New York I got a postcard, a map of the world and it said on the back: 'Sweetie, "God does not intend us all to be rich, or powerful or great, but he does intend us all to be friends." Ralph Waldo Emerson. Don't you dare give up on the world. It's not allowed – IF [writ large] IF you believe in God. Love, your Nana.'

# 7

# The Other Side of Her Door

♣ ♦ ♥ ♠

ONCE WHEN WE WERE VISITING, THE DOORBELL rang and a man stood, hat in hand, mumbling, bowing, and asking for money, for work or just for food. The two or three of us who answered the doorbell stood there like bumps on a log, having run to the door; not knowing what to do or say, except to yell: 'Nana! Nana! Someone's at the door.' She came running, or as close to it as I ever saw her, hearing the edge in our voices. As soon as she rounded the corner and the man came into view she smiled warmly and invited him in. She sat him at the dining room table and plied him with bread, a glass of milk and said it would take her a few minutes to heat up the leftovers from yesterday's dinner.

Rootling around in the kitchen, fridge door opening, shutting, the oven, the quick smell of the gas lit, plates rattling, silverware out of the drawer and she kept coming to the doorway, smiling encouragingly at him and talking. Simple things any child would respond to, but respectful. Where was he from? Was he just passing through, going any place in particular? What kind of work might interest him? Then as the food warmed she led him into the kitchen to wash his hands and face with one of her best guest towels. And then she served him, asking him if it was enough. More meat, gravy? Then she served pie and coffee and sat with him and had her tea.

She introduced each of us to him in turn and we came forward awkwardly and sort of nodded and then stepped back and stood at the edge of the room watching and listening, wondering who he was and why Nana was treating him like a lost relative, using the good china and silver, and asking about him and his family. She'd said, 'Here, take a load off your feet' and then suggested perhaps he'd like to take a nap but he only stayed a few minutes after he'd eaten. And Nana seemed to know that would be the case because she'd made up a bag for him, sandwiches, two apples, cookies, saltines, a bar of soap and washcloth, a razor, a pair of socks and a holy card with a picture of a man with a dog – who I later found out was the patron saint of travellers – those we'd probably call transients, the homeless or just bums. It was St Roque who always travelled the roads and shared his food with strangers, making them friends and tending to their hurts, cuts and wounds, both inner and more obvious. He would pick up stray dogs and feed them from what he begged from others. They were good company as he travelled his way, befriending others forced to be pilgrims and travellers by poverty or violence. She walked him to the door, shook his hand and watched him go down the front steps and on his way.

We were immediately all over her, asking questions: Who was he? Did she know him and on and on? She sat in her rocker and talked with us, saying quietly: 'Such a sad man; such a sad thing.' She looked at us and asked: 'Did you see it in his eyes?' We'd seen his shabby clothes and torn shoes, his ratty hair and how he smelled, old and dirty. 'He's "touched",' you know?' No, we didn't know. Touched by who? 'Oh,' she said, oddly as though no one was listening to her and she was repeating something old from way back when she was little – 'the porch light is on but nobody much is home anymore. So sad. He's a lost soul.' The looks on our faces just then told her we were very interested in who he was but hadn't a clue what she was talking about.

She abruptly changed tactics in explaining. 'Sometimes folks get hurt terribly. Something happens to them and it effects them so much that they're never quite the same again. They are physically hurt or they grieve a death, or lose someone they love, or they see evil and violence up close, something no one should have to see and part of them just breaks. So part of them goes away, or goes to sleep but they keep walking around and have to live.'

'Your body is like a house and when these things happen to you, it's like the house is empty and your soul goes wandering off. It comes back on occasion but sometimes you spend the rest of your life like that man. That's what I mean when I say he's "touched" – like getting burned but there's no scar or mark – the wound is inside. You must be very kind to them, be respectful – you never know who they were, who they really are. My mother used to say, in Ireland – when they'd come to our back door, that God had a habit of visiting the earth, or an angel – like the kings of old that would go in disguise to see what the people were really like. And the way you treated them, "the touched", would be the way you really were at heart.'

Immediately one of us asked if that had been God? She smiled and said, 'I dunna know for sure. You never do.' I said: 'But he was so sad, so empty and he didn't say anything practically, not even "thank you".' 'Oh yes he did,' she said quickly, 'he accepted everything so graciously. He ate slowly and enjoyed it; he bowed to me on the way out and when he took what little I gave him I could tell. And his handshake was strong – some of him was still at home inside while he was here. You didn't see, but you learn to tell after a while.'

We wanted to know how he got that way, blunt as children can be. 'It's awful to live with something either you did or someone else did to you. And worst of all is to have to do it alone. I used to think the worst thing was to have no one to share your troubles with, your sorrow and your fears, a tragedy or a loss, but now I know that the worst is to have no one to share your joys and your soul with, no one to laugh with – it's a terrible ache, a pity.'

Again that distant look that made her seem sad at moments when she didn't think anyone was watching her, like in the early morning before anyone else got up. She was always sitting in her rocking chair, quiet, moving to a steady rhythm and at times crying so softly – and then it hit me hard that she was talking about herself too. She was alone. Oh, she had us to come visit her and one of our aunts lived with her and she came home from work every evening, but she'd been a widow for a long time. I was eleven maybe, then, and Grandpa had died long before I was born. For the first time I knew she was lonely. Being alone, outliving or losing who you love – and having no one to share your joy with – so much worse than going through the hard stuff alone – it sunk in deep. That's when I began to know that a friend is someone to share your joy with, but even more, a friend was someone who could rejoice in your good times and lift you, give you a reason to rejoice when there was none. What a loss not to have known my grandfather – who had been her joy! As she had been his – and was ours!

# 8

# *Geraniums*

♣  ♦  ♥  ♠

I N SOME OF THE WINDOWS IN NANA'S APARTMENT THERE were deep recesses and in every single one of them were pots of geraniums – not plants like you see in flower shops or gardens or nurseries, but huge, sprawling, strange-shaped geraniums. Some were squat and fell over the ledge but mostly they climbed like ivy – stalks twisted, long-curved, in every direction possible (from being turned regularly to get the full rays of the sun). She doted on those flowers – would sing to them when she watered them, talk to them when she picked off the dry leaves and pinched a stem here and there or crumbled a flower that had dried up and was falling all over the counter.

She told me once that those plants, (which were considered downright ugly and deformed by most folk … and I'd let that thought cross my mind a couple of times), those plants were her shelter – her refuge from the cold of winter. They kept her going through the long grey months of November into April. And they were full of life, colour, even smell – a very distinct, unique smell, textures with the leaves almost tough and gritty. They had to be tough in order to survive. Those window sills were cold and only knew sun for a couple of hours each day, but they made it. She would close the curtain behind them, up against the window panes so that the plants stood inside what warmth the curtains gave at night.

They flowered profusely and were an incredibly healthy rich green, with huge fat stems. And colours – pink and 'geranium' red of course. But their roots had twisted in around each other and pieces had been transplanted from pot to pot and so there were white ones, reds tinged with pink interiors and white edges, pinks with deep blood red centres and pale almost translucent pinks and hybrids – weird and wonderful wild geraniums in every window that could catch a bit of sunlight slanting through paned, crossed windows and sliding through the buildings outside. The ones in the front of the brownstone were the most unusual shapes. Her geraniums didn't look like any I'd ever seen before (though I did notice soon after that my mother's had that same ragged look to them in parts of our house and I thought that this was her shelter too, her refuge in the midst of winter on the east coast and maybe from all of the housework and care of so many of us kids). Strange how slow we are to see what's under our noses. Just one moment of seeing something elsewhere suddenly clears the film from our eyes and what's close to home jumps out at us.

I wanted to grow some geraniums of my own and wanted Nana to give me cuttings. I'd even picked out which ones I would start with (the ones I thought were the prettiest or the strongest colours) and I was sure I could do it easily enough. It couldn't be that hard to grow them. They were tough. So I asked. I got more than cuttings to start in my own pots at home. We began with one to practice on while I was visiting. I got tough seeds that were planted into the young soil of my soul and the planting or the transplanting wasn't as easy as I'd thought it would be.

She was delighted that I wanted to try gardening geraniums. 'It's an art,' she said 'and it takes time and practice and patience and it tells you a lot about yourself – often what you'd prefer not to know.' She said: 'I'll start with two cuttings' and she deftly cut off a piece from the scraggliest plant – not one I'd have picked. She saw the look on my face and laughed. 'Then we prepare the soil in a small pot. Now you have to know that when you plant seeds or a cutting you're also working on yourself. I'm going to tell you what my mother told me when I did my first cutting. Here it is – "Just because someone is crazy or grumpy or plain nasty, or odd, doesn't mean that what they say to you – or about you – isn't actually true!"'

I never could figure out where these lines came from or what actually triggered them – or if she waited and bided her time to spring them on me. But I wisely, for the moment, didn't say anything and kept my mouth shut.

She went on patting the soil, making sure it was deep enough. 'You know, none of us take criticism well, and we don't like to be corrected, or to be disagreed with. Often we decide that we don't like the look of them or they're not worthwhile – so we don't pay them any mind.' As she rambled on, I realised I was getting annoyed. What was she saying about me or what I would have chosen – or worse?

'Ok, now,' she said. 'You do the next one. Did you watch how I cut the stem.' Quickly, somehow to redeem myself I said, 'Yes' and took the scissors. I could be as deft and sure as she was. She let me cut and then looked at it knowingly and said: 'That one won't take well. You didn't see where I cut it. This one is cut at a point below where the leaves intersect.' I was getting more annoyed. I tried again and then began to push it into the soil. 'Easy, easy, make a hole with your fingers and put it in like you're putting something you love to bed – it's going to stay where you put it for a long time – until it dies or is thrown out or you transplant it.' Again I tried working at it – it had looked so easy initially.

And as I was patting down the soil she spoke again. 'Ok, here's the second thing you're transplanting – exactly what I was told a long time ago. Just because you're angry at someone doesn't mean that they actually did anything wrong!' I was taken aback – how did she know what I was feeling? She looked at me and went on – 'More often than not, when we get angry it's because we're annoyed with ourselves, not the other person. They just happen to be the place where we caught a glimpse of ourselves in an unflattering light.'

I thought – how did she know all these things? And then looking at the clutter, the sprawling geraniums in just this one window I thought – very uncharacteristically – there is so much to learn! I was just starting.

'Tomorrow,' she said, 'we'll talk about the colours of the flowers and what you mix to get those colours and then how to come up with something you've never seen before! With geraniums you never know – they're grand that way!' Then I got kissed on the forehead and my braids tugged a bit. She went back to her work and off I went, not angry anymore and thinking, I wonder if parts of me are that scraggly and yet beautiful inside. Nothing Nana seems to see in me bothers her.

And now the sight of the geraniums questions me further. Am I shelter for someone in grey light, against winter's cold stare? Strange, as I have grown all these years, like her, like all of us, that is what's most important – to be shelter for one another and refuge in the face of ordinary wear and tear on our souls. Ah geraniums!

Now, in my sixties, I'm delighted to report that my geraniums are just as scraggly, huge, and weirdly lovely. The green thumb has been passed on.

## — 9 —

# The Jester's Prayer

♣    ◆    ♥    ♠

I WAS A VORACIOUS READER FROM A YOUNG AGE. I LEARNED to read when I was three or so, tracing out the letters and numbers. If I answered the phone I had to be able to listen carefully and repeat back, out loud, the string of numbers and call letters the voice on the other end was reading or quoting me from the Exhange (my dad became a financial analyst). Books had been gifts since I was too young to even know it was a book – made of cloth, then big pictures and few words, if any. Alphabet books, counting and rhymes, then pop-ups and then *real* books, no pictures, just words. My dad would stop in a second-hand bookstore every Friday night in downtown DC on his way home and pick up a box of books for a couple of bucks. You never knew what you'd get: mysteries, westerns, historical novels, science fiction, kids' books, colouring books, a single volume of an encyclopædia, junk, but sometimes a classic like *Little Women,* or a *Tom Sawyer* or *The Hardy Girls* mysteries. They would keep me somewhat engaged for the week.

I had been exploring, discovering and escaping into the world of books and open pages for over a decade – I'd even built myself a 'lair' of books in the basement when Nana gave me my best book ever. It was old, but in great condition, hard bound with gold embossing. It was illustrated, but not with pictures, in black and white, with borders for certain title pages and tiny engravings at the end of chapters. The first edition was published in Ireland in 1874 and that made it special to begin with. It was the oldest book I owned and somehow older was better, rarer, and so to be treasured. And best of all, it had been Nana's since she was young. It was entitled *The Jester's Prayer,* a medieval legend of a jester, who juggled and sang, walked a tightrope, danced, did somersaults, stood on his head, walked on his hands and told jokes — ribald ones (I learned that word, along with bawdy) — and stories of travelling with a troupe across France and Europe — even to Russia and Turkey. I loved the story and read it over and over again and it became one of the first stories I learned 'by heart' to actually tell aloud to others.

The jester grew older and requested shelter at a monastery where he had performed a number of times. The abbot remembered him and granted his request not because he felt sorry for him but because he had brought revelry and laughter to the town and the monastery during a hard winter in a time of famine. The man settled in — room, meals, prayers, but he really didn't fit. He couldn't read and so couldn't pray along with the monks. He had no work to do when all the others went to their assigned tasks. He wandered forlornly through the out-buildings, gardens, granaries and the great cathedral beside the monastery. And one day in a small alcove in the basement, among cold stonewalls and floors he found a statue. It had once been richly handpainted and adorned and its clothes covered in gold leaf in better days, but that was long ago. The Lady was dirty, dusty, chipped, with huge gouges in the folds of her gown and even her face was dented. She held a child of about two years old who had once held the world — it was missing along with her right hand. She looked like he felt, he thought.

He had nothing else to do so cleaned her up and then had a crazy idea — he'd entertain her and the child. So, he started slipping away, out of sight of the other monks who he was sure wouldn't understand — perhaps they even resented his being there and doing nothing already. He gathered his props, hidden in a bag under his bed. He knew he was out of shape but he hung the tightrope across the alcove and got on and fell off and got on again, until it came back to him. Then he came

walking on his hands, doing tumbling tricks, juggling everything from balls, to swords, and eating an apple at the same
time! And he sang – softly so no one would hear him – the old
songs, and told them jokes – the ribald ones! And every night
he was exhausted, suffering from aches and pains, but content
at last. Now he had his work to do but he was always afraid of
getting caught.

That fear was well-based, sadly enough. There's always
someone who self-righteously and religiously looks to find
something wrong, to trip another up and this monastery had
its busybody who followed the old man, intent on finding out
what he was up to. He was shocked! He watched it all and then
reported it in detail to the abbot.

The abbot was dismayed. If this was true he'd have to let the
old man go – the next day he and the monk who had reported
him slipped down to the cathedral basement and hid behind
pillars and waited. His heart sank as he watched the old man
and his feeble attempts at singing, and the awful jokes and
juggling, and walking on his hands, and on the tightrope. It was
unseemly – he'd have to dismiss him immediately.

He was about to come out from his hiding place when the old
jester slipped and fell off the tightrope and lay unconscious on
the floor. The abbot moved, but another moved more quickly.
He froze and watched as the statue, the Lady, stirred and
stepped nimbly down from her pedestal, child in hand. She
placed the child down on the floor and went over and bent
over the old man, solicitous and kind. She lifted the hem of
her dirty old dress and carefully wiped the sweat from his face
and leaned down to kiss him on his forehead.

The child played with the juggling balls and swords and
then when no one was looking – or so he thought – he surrep-
titiously put one of the brightly coloured balls into his sleeve.
The Lady rose, picked him up and leapt easily, gracefully, like
an acrobat herself, back up onto her pedestal and was wood
again. The child sat in her one good crooked arm but now
there was a faint smile on his face and in his hand a gloriously
bright blue ball.

The next day the jester was summoned to the abbot's quarters.
He was terrified, sure he was to be expelled, but the abbot told

him and calmed his fears – I know what you're doing and I now assign you to that work, as long as you are able. The old jester's life couldn't have been better. He left rejoicing and the years went on and on. It came to pass that the jester could no longer juggle or walk the tightrope. He couldn't even get down to the Lady's Chapel. The abbot would come every evening and sit with the older man reading to him, praying and singing with him. And then one night while the abbot dozed off the Lady and the baby came again. Half asleep he saw her take the end of her skirt and wipe the jester's brow again, and she sang softly to him, kissed him and took him home. The small boy handed his filched bright blue ball to the abbot as he went with his mother.

They say the abbot learned to juggle, could last only a few seconds on the tightrope but could tumble reasonably well. And he wrote many songs to the Lady and the Child who played with the world. He stood in for the jester as long as he could. Some say he became a great saint, Bernard of Clairvaux – that's what some say

There was something about the story, the illustrations depicting the late middle ages and the fact that Nana had read it and kept it all those years and now was passing it on to me. When she asked me why I liked the book, I had trouble putting words around it. I began: 'Oh I know it never really happened that way, but'… and trailed off at a loss for words. And then, of course, she put it into words perfectly – just what I couldn't reach for with my mind or my too young heart.

'Don't you want to do something for God that no one else has ever done before – but God's been waiting forever for someone to dare to do just *that?*' Yes, that was it. We both sat there thinking, until I thought she'd fallen asleep – but she added – 'you certainly don't want to be like that mean old monk whose heart was so shrivelled up no matter what his age – do you?' 'Of course not,' she answered herself. I still mull over that question that has often become my prayer – that work that no one else will ever do – my work, is it awaiting me and God waiting for me to dream it and do it? Is this what I spend my life doing? (sigh)

# *History*

♣　♦　♥　♠

I HAD FOUND A GREAT LINE JUST MONTHS BEFORE NANA died while writing a paper on God – a Jewish quote from Martin Buber (though I cannot cite the source so many years later). It read: 'God is always speaking, but he never repeats himself, like sunrises and sunsets.' It was a great one-liner and I shared it with Nana. She was still as sharp as ever and smiled very knowingly and I thought, hmmmm, Buber and Nana would make good friends – now that would be a conversation and meeting, a dialogue that I'd love to be a fly on the wall to overhear!

After a few moments she spoke. 'It's true. God speaks in everything, people, relationships, even all that dies, but sometimes, I've learned, God speaks very, very, very slowly – like in history and through a long war when so few resisted. They just took turns at killing. Or in your own life – only looking back do you hear where it was music and where it was so right and good and just – and sometimes you have to wait until forever until you can hear what was being said, let alone understand it, or see where it fit in with everything else. Sometimes, for a while, it sounds like screaming or wailing, mourning or it's just silence, so empty, you wonder if there's anything or anyone there – out there or in here.'

'In the meantime though, you have to stake your life on a dearer, truer hope and live as though it's already all redeemed even though you're just trying hard to believe and hang in there. It has to be *all* music to God's ears and to our ears too — it's getting tuned to how *slowly* God talks to us and to all the world, that is the trick ... So, so, slowly ...'

— 11 —

# All Souls' Day, November 2

♣  ♦  ♥  ♠

ONE ALL SOULS' DAY, THE DAY AFTER ALL SAINTS'
Day, I took Nana back from church and she
asked me to read to her one of the readings from
Scripture, from the Old Testament book of Daniel,
because she didn't remember it as what was read out in
church. I obliged – it was about stars in the firmament and
those who are faithful and shining, out-shining those stars
when they have died.

> At that time there shall arise
> Michael, the great prince,
> Guardian of your people;
> It shall be a time unsurpassed in distress since nations
>     began
> until that time. At that time your people shall escape,
>     everyone
> who is found written in the book.
>
> Many of those who sleep in the dust of the earth shall
>     awake;
> Some shall live forever, others shall be an everlasting
>     horror
>  and disgrace.
> But the wise shall shine brightly like the splendour of
>     the firmament,

And those who lead the many to justice shall be like
the stars forever.
— Daniel 12:1-3

After she had listened and was quiet for a while she repeated
a line I'd heard her say since I was very young. 'You know,' she
said, 'Only those who walk in darkness ever see the stars.' She
went on, talking half to herself and to me, and nobody at all –
'Did you ever wonder what happens to stars? Do they die? Do
they burn out exhausted? Do they fall into a black hole?' I
knew she wasn't looking for a response from me, and certainly
not on scientific terms. I kept quiet, waiting to see where this
would go. 'Did you ever watch a shooting star as it falls
through the night? You know they're really angels – the stars.
And when a star falls or becomes a shooting star it's because
they were given a choice – to give up being an angel – to give
their life, their light to those who need it on earth – and if they
do – they're allowed to go out in glory.'

'Many do but have no witness. No one sees them because
we're not looking, scanning the sky and marvelling at the
Creator's hand. However, they do it anyway and anyone
who's lucky enough to catch it – that moment of delight and
surprise – Ah! They know that for just that moment in the
pitch darkness, life and love redeemed someone, something,
somewhere. And once you see it, you have to imitate the stars,
the angels in their heavens, and us here on earth.'

'Maybe resurrection for us is like those angels, those stars
shooting like beacons, like night lights across the sky – that's
the way to go out.' A long pause ensued. 'That's the way I'm
going to go out. That's the way I'm going home, just like it says
in the book of Daniel.'

Four decades after she died someone sent me a card with a
line from the Sufi poet Rumi: 'If you are here unfaithfully with
us you're causing terrible damage.' And I can't help but try to
frame its opposite, using Nana's words and beliefs – 'If you are
here among us faithfully, you're redeeming us all and blessing
us with wisdom and grace.'

# The Pickle Barrel, Pickle Puckering

♣　♦　♥　♠

IT WAS A JEWISH NEIGHBOURHOOD FOR A LONG TIME, on the edge, just past the streets of the Irish, Italian and German neighbourhoods. We drifted there – at least the kids did, picking up phrases of the languages of our school friends: Yiddish, Ukranian, Gaelic, Polish – the really important things you had to know how to say in a half-dozen languages:

♣ Do you want to stay over tonight?
♦ My mom said it's OK.
♥ Do you want to have dinner with us?
♠ Do you want to come back and study with me?
♣ Mom, this is my friend …
♦ Dad, I want you to meet …

And you had to know, on a first name basis, which you never used, their parents, like they knew yours. They felt perfectly free to correct you, discipline you and sometimes, for really serious infractions, tell one of your parents.

There were crucial people in the neighbourhood: the butcher, the baker, the pickle man, the grinder, the fish seller, your godparents and your friends' godparents. It was the pickle man I visited every Sunday morning after church. He had the best kosher pickles anywhere (though *my* experience was severely limited). There was a huge barrel where you could pick your own, with tongs. It would be wrapped in wax paper and off I'd go happy as a lark – grimacing and taking bites out of it, the more sour the better. You ate it with your mouth and hands, but your whole face screwed up if it was really dill, really a good pickle.

Nana would look at my face and say seriously: 'Better watch it or your face might get stuck that way! Isn't it strange that something that can twist and contort your face and pucker you up can be so good? Pucker up, sweetie, I'm coming for a kisser.'

There would be plenty of times that what could comfort you and twist your heart would still end up being able to pucker you up for a kiss (kiss or be kissed!). She had her favourites: martinis, scotch, Irish whiskey, blackberry liquor (all for medicinal purposes of course – hot toddies and before bedtime to help you sleep); the smell of certain flowers – the wilder, the stronger the odour, sauerkraut, getting kissed by anyone you didn't really know, like 'kissing' cousins at wakes and funerals … or anyone you kissed, really kissed for the first time … or anyone you loved, who could make you cry. To this day there are certain smells and tastes that make me smile and I think: 'Pucker up sweetie, I'm coming for a kisser' and I find myself looking around for someone, anyone to kiss! – just to stay in shape.

— 13 —

# No Accounting for Taste in the Human Race

♣　♦　♥　♠

**On Matters of the Heart**

It was the sixties in New York and I'd fallen in love. My folks had come up from DC to meet him and I was nervous, very nervous, and we were all at Nana's house before going into Manhattan for dinner to meet him. My mom was in the shower and my dad was reading the paper and I was talking to him, trying to tell them a few pieces of crucial information before we left. Nana was in the kitchen. I went through a list of what he'd done, where he worked, his talents – great twelve string guitarist, from Louisiana and, I slipped it in – he's black. No response. My dad wasn't really listening. I tried it again and towards the end of the litany said it a little slower and louder: he's black. It was my mother who heard from the shower and came out dripping wet, yelling at my father: 'Did you hear what she said?' – he hadn't. And it started. And it wasn't a good morning.

I retreated to the kitchen in tears, wanting Nana to say something. She did, as always and took me by surprise. She stood by the sink, wiped her hands on her apron and declared: 'Honey, there is no accounting for taste in the human race. Don't let others decide for you – the crucial bits are all yours. You're going to live with your choices and their consequences. You're not marrying his parents or your parents. You're marry-

[55]

ing him. Only your heart can give you certain answers. No one else can. Just remember this marriage thing is for forever, for always, all ways until forever – and there's no waffling allowed.'

'The Jewish people have a saying; I've heard them quoting it in matters of the heart – "souls must mingle tears" – that's the person you marry – the one who you not only can cry with but just catching sight of them, being in their presence, can move you to tears – for any reason, but especially just for the fact that they are and they are in your world and you decide to belong to each other.'

'There are some things that are worth losing everything for – even your family – there are very few, but love and deep abiding friendship is one of them. And if you're friends, good friends, your marriage will last forever, in spite of it all, no matter what.'

She went on: 'It's my fault anyway [I knew my folks were listening in the living room – she was talking loud enough for them to hear]. So he's black. What, you aren't? Didn't you know you're black Irish from the north, girl? It's my fault. I'll talk to your mother and dad – it was me who told you to go find someone tall, dark and handsome and you were just being a good obedient granddaughter. Besides,' she said, smiling at me, 'you did good' (she had met him already). And I had to smile, even chuckle through and in spite of my tears. It was time to go to dinner.

# 14

# On Loving

♣  ♦  ♥  ♠

M Y NANA WAS BORN OCTOBER 9. MY DAD WAS born October 9. Wow! I thought, what a gift to get on your Mom's birthday – what a gift to give on your birthday! I always thought there was somehow a special connection between them. It got me to thinking about the gift of life I was given by my mother who was twenty-nine when she gave birth to me. It must have been daunting since I was number four and she'd lost two full term babies between my older sister and me. And my Dad was away in the war, in the South Pacific. I have a picture of him, on the day that I was born, on the deck of his ship, sailing from Samoa to Guam, 25 October 1944. She wouldn't see him until February and then, just for two days in San Francisco.

Probably in my early forties (I come late in life to some really good ideas) I chanced upon the ritual of giving – sending flowers to my Mother on my birthday in sheer gratitude for life – no matter what had transpired that year, it was grand and as I grew older I became more and more inordinately attached to giving. The first time I sent the flowers, she was startled, even stunned – but she loved it. It made a stir in the family. After that it was a ritual, connective tissue between my mother and me. I'd look for flowers that said something about the year that had just passed – an orchid that bloomed for weeks on end, a gardenia or a jasmine plant with a rich odour, pots and pots of impatience that she put on the front porch –

one of her perennial favourites and of course, long stem roses, of many colours: deep red, soft pinks, pure whites, yellow butters, even grey mauves ... or wildflowers – carpets to lay out in the backyard and a basket of what they'd look like to pick when they bloomed. There were azaleas to plant and iris, glads, bluebells and bonnets – it was as much the choice as the giving of it that we both looked forward to over the years.

I never thought to do it for my father – or to extend it back a generation to the only grandparent I had, Nana! Amazing how blinkered we can be, in our gifting and learning to appreciate those who have given so much to us – and they sadly go unsung and unnoticed for decades.

Well Nana heard of the ritual – it was the talk of a number of family members and she brought it up at breakfast one morning when I was visiting her. She eyed me over the oatmeal (a standard, from October to May, Navy variety – really bad stuff not to be redeemed by brown sugar, dried fruit, anything. Even the dog wouldn't eat the stuff) and coffee. 'Right pleased with yourself aren't you?' She caught me off-guard. It was early morning and my brain hadn't kicked in yet. I was still in what I refer to as 'low grade life form'. 'Huh?' 'The flowers,' she said smiling, 'it was a good, grand gesture', which was akin to high praise in her book. I grinned. However, she had more to say ...

She'd been reading the newspapers and she gestured toward a story – famine widespread in a remote country in Africa. 'It's woeful that so many do without and others have so much excess to share. I remember what it was like not to have anything extra to give to the people you loved, even in your own family. If you gave something, it meant you did without it yourself – it was hard – but you knew the worth of the gift in terms other than money. In fact – the worth of the gift isn't its price but the lack it engenders in the giver.' I was stunned. I'd studied theology for years – an odd profession and way of making ends meet, technically studying 'God' and all in relation to Divinity which covers a multitude of areas like justice, ethics, peace, prayer and the Scriptures for starters. And never had I heard the act of giving or sacrifice so astutely put. But she wasn't finished.

'You know – family isn't everything. You have to learn to love other people's children and relatives at least as much as you do your own.' Among other members of my kin those would be seen as fighting words, akin to heresy. 'But – that's what you do, what you have to do if you're Catholic. After all the word itself means "universal" – everyone everywhere all the time, even your enemies, but especially those that lack the most. I'm sure that it's the poor – those without who still manage to live with grace and hospitality with others who somehow save us all – and we don't even suspect them of giving us *that* gift!' She never ceased to amaze me – where did she get this stuff. These profound insights, she could, if need be I was sure, hold her own with any theologian or philosopher worth their salt and go head to toe with them, and best them!

I had been silent too long and she poked at me, throwing out the bait – 'You do believe in the Incarnation don't you?' 'Of course I do!' 'Well dearie,' she said, 'look around' and she gestured towards the street that was crowded with folks on their way to work, then to the newspaper with its front page picture of crowds of starving refugees thin as rails and then she gestured in a circle to the world at large – 'this is as good as it gets!'

I was fast trying to reconstruct the pattern of her logic. Her thoughts were like the diagram of a molecule – all these diverse pieces interconnected, all one. I was back at the Incarnation question. I started thinking out loud. 'Incarnation is God becoming human, being both God and human, one of us. So all we know of God in human terms we can see, hear and know in Jesus.' She interrupted me. 'But do you believe it? God is one of us. He stayed. He dwells with us – the Body of Christ – look around – it's everyone. All those people outside on the street, those people in Africa – not just your small circle – it's billions and billions of them – and because of the Incarnation, whatever we do to and for anyone of them, our God takes personally that we were gifting him, and whatever we don't do for them, when we ignore them, when they're in distress – we ignore God.' (Matthew 25's parable of the sheep and goats, Nana's version.)

I'd never heard it put so bluntly, so succinctly before. But it was her last line that tore open a rift in my mind. It was very soft spoken and I had to strain, leaning forward to catch the words – she was over eighty by now. 'I wonder if anyone ever gave them flowers – or a feast [she was pointing to the people in Africa on the front page of the *Times*] – now, *that* would be as good as it gets, wouldn't it?' Those words I've had to live with since she spoke them and I was the only one to hear.

# 15

# Nana's Prayer Book

♣ ♦ ♥ ♠

NANA HAD AN OLD PRAYER BOOK, ONCE WHITE (from her wedding day). The pages were browning on the edges, yellowing and frayed. The leather was so worn it was soft to the touch. And it expanded with the years, crammed with holy cards – first communions, confirmations, for all the grandkids, some ordination cards, but mostly as time went on, it was stuffed with remembrance cards. They gave a name, date of birth and death, the years lived, usually with the line, 'May the souls of the faithful departed, rest in peace. Amen' along with a cross. The front of the card was a standard picture of the Good Shepherd, Mary, the saints, an angel, or the crucifixion (I always looked for one that would depict the resurrection). They were her neighbours, cousins, dear friends, church acquaintances, names even she had forgotten along with their faces or their connection to her, but she still prayed for them. And there were newspaper clippings of total strangers (she read the Obit page daily and would take out the ones who had no surviving relatives, considering them to be bereft with no one to pray for them).

For decades she'd trudged to church in the evenings in clement weather and inclement times, even in plain miserable weathers for devotions. I asked her once: 'Don't you get tired of praying for the same people over and over again?' I'd hear her mouth the names outloud but so low it sounded like a hum or a murmur. It was her personal litany that encompassed her world but what I didn't realise was how vast her world was – how it ambled back in time and how crowded her heart was – always with room for more – for another soul, another *name*.

It was when we went home later that evening that she answered my query. I didn't go to devotions much, mostly only when I went to visit her. She started by asking me questions. This had gotten to be a routine since she knew I was studying theology – she would have stirred second thoughts into anyone who thought they knew what they were talking about when they were talking about God! It was in the seventies and in the throes of the Vietnam war and I was involved in boycotts, protests, peace marches, civil disobedience and the like. She started straight in – 'Who do you pray for when you're picketing and marching and not singing?' It hadn't even crossed my mind to do anything of the sort, except for Francis of Assisi's Peace Prayer or an Our Father so I wouldn't react negatively to someone.

'Well, do you pray for the soldiers? Our soldiers, their soldiers, and all those people? We're busy killing millions of them – so many more than ours – I watch that body count every morning on TV. Do you pray for our leaders and their leaders? If only someone would bring up the topic of negotiations again. Just because we started fighting doesn't mean you have to keep at it until there's no one left – do you pray for all the people who don't agree with you and shout obscenities and those awful things at you, cursing you as they go by and giving you the finger?' Here she was in her eighties and she was aware of so much. I hadn't realised she knew what was going on in the world, or that it touched her so deeply.

She raised her eyebrows and said: 'What do you think I'm praying for at all those devotions? You don't use prayer or devotions to avoid people and your responsibilities to them – or to avoid the big tasks like being a peacemaker. You use the devotion and the prayers to help you face the hard stuff, to "love your enemies" and pray for those who persecute you and do you harm, blessing them instead of nursing your anger and thinking of ways to hurt them back, in your heart. If you're supposed to love your enemies, you'd better well know who you think they are!' (paraphrase of Luke's sermon on the plain according to Nana).

'You're supposed to be praying always and not lose heart, aren't you? It says that somewhere in the gospel doesn't it?' [Luke 18 and she's the widow going after the judge in Jesus' story, in league with all the other widows and orphans, and the poor, and Jesus himself!] 'After all you never know who you're going to meet in heaven.'

I thought that last line was a quantum leap in the thought patterns there. 'What do you mean?' I countered back. She eyed me over her granny glasses, perched on the end of her nose, with infinite patience, as though teaching someone very slow the alphabet or numbers. 'Who's the first person you're going to meet when you get to those pearly gates, sweetie?' I thought she was putting me on. I ventured ... Saint Peter? 'No way,' she said – 'you'll be introduced to the person who got you in!' I was flabbergasted. But the next question and answer bothered me more – and still does. 'And do you know who's the second person who'll be waiting for you?' 'No,' I gulped out. 'The person you almost kept out, that's who!' 'Think of it,' she said, 'it could be so many people – both of them. I'm making sure I'm friends with as many of them as I can before I die! You never know who might be a friend of God – a much better friend of God's than you ever were!'

She died at eighty-six having made sure everyone around her mourned her going, but I wouldn't be surprised if she's the one who gets me in – or perhaps that's just pietistic dreaming on my part, ignoring her words about others being as important as family. And I don't want to devalue any of her words and life. Perhaps I'll be entirely stunned at who stands welcome at those gates, recognising and waiting for me to come home, announcing: 'Come in – you are very welcome here!' And I would never have pegged them, him or her, as the one who made sure I got in! Never!

# 16

# Brownies – Comfort Food

♣ ♦ ♥ ♠

**B**ROWNIES! JUST THE SOUND OF THE WORD IN my mouth makes me smile – in remembering and repeated anticipations. The word feels rich, chewy, dense, dark, sweet. My father made them mostly – and then we learned. It's Nana's best recipe! Even the page that carried the ingredients and directions, the amounts needed, was smudged with fingerprints of old batter (now it's on an index card with more of the same) but now I know it by heart too.

My dad would say – on a Saturday afternoon or sometimes on a Friday night – 'I think I'll make Nana's brownies' – and everything stopped! We'd all traipse off to the kitchen, which was probably one of the smallest rooms in the house and the one I remember most. And we'd begin to round up the ingredients. There was the long rectangular and a short square pan (one for walnuts and one without). And we watched. Sometimes we'd ask a question. Then we waited. It was the batter-lined bowl that we all coveted – and a spatula so that not one little bit would be left on the inside of that bowl when it was put into the sink to wash. Any little splatter on the table, the counter top (even the floor) was quickly removed with a deft finger and a lick.

Who got to lick the bowl? It followed different routines. Sometimes it went from the oldest to the youngest or the reverse – each got one lick. Or all the girls went first, then the boys (usually a six to three ratio depending on who was home, or around). There was often a good bit of grousing when it seemed someone cheated and took more than one good swipe. Best of all was when dad (or, even more rarely, Nana) would single out just one of us and say 'wanna make brownies?' Then you got to lick the whole bowl all by yourself — besides a big teaspoon of batter (you were given the latitude and we always thought we were getting away with something, though, of course we weren't!)

Then we waited while they baked — and then there was another wait. They had to cool at least forty-five to fifty minutes in the pan or else they came out in pieces; wet and moist, sticking to the pan. They had to be tested. A straw inserted into the middle had to come out squeaky clean and then the mixture would be divided and cut into pieces with long, sure and deft cuts, across and down.

The trick to really good brownies (our tradition) was a bit flakey on the top crust and soft and chewy inside. The best pieces, in my humble opinion, were the ends, or more precisely the corners — you got both the flake and crunch and the soft insides — best of both. I was partial to the ones with nuts (luckily I shared that with Nana and dad, but a lot of the others didn't like them). The walnuts usually had to be cracked, shelled and the meat picked out as carefully as you could, the bigger the pieces, the more intact the nuts, the better. That pan mixture was more labour-intensive than the plain chocolate ones.

And the chocolate had to be semi-sweet baking chocolate, not milk chocolate. It was crucial to the taste somehow. Now when I make them I try to use 70 per cent cocoa or even more, the darker the better. And then came the eating. The first ones we all ate together. And silence prevailed except for sensuous sounds of delicious and pure pleasure and enjoyment being prolonged. Maybe we got two each that first cutting and sharing. Then tinfoil was put over the pan. They were left until all were gone.

From then on — my dad guarded them! Everyone, including him, was wont — at any hour of the day or night — to try and steal one or two (that was real daring). It took skill to extract the brownie, quiet stealth and not get caught eating it! With upwards of eleven people in a small house at any one time this was not as easy as you might think. The kitchen was right smack in the middle of the house, a thoroughfare – and everyone was usually thinking of how to get another brownie. Sometimes (when one of us was really clever) we'd take a knife and slit the whole row – a thin cut, along the length of the pan (and not so noticeable unless you'd done it a couple of times). It gave great satisfaction to know you'd outwitted everyone (unless you got caught – then you were supposed to lose your turn at licking the bowl next time around).

The process of making, the waiting, the ritual cutting and division, the shared-in goodness, the sheer taste of togetherness, and then sometimes the stealing of more, all added up to more than a tradition or a memory. It became what is now often called a comfort food. Taste was important, of course, but it was so much more.

Once – I figure I might have been twelve or thirteen (nowhere for a young girl in the 1950s) – I was making brownies with Nana at her house in New York – that in itself was a rarity to be treasured. I was picking at the batter. Why is it that it's as good uncooked as cooked!? Finally Nana said: 'Enough is enough! Why don't you eat the whole bowl?' I was stunned and couldn't believe my good fortune. I had just lucked out!

And I did – slowly savouring every tablespoon, finger and bit on the spatula and bowl – and I learned something hard for anyone to believe – or two things really. First – you can have too much sweetness! And then, more importantly – it isn't the same when you eat certain foods alone. The most important part of the taste is other people!

I didn't feel too well the rest of the afternoon, drinking milk to ease the cloying sweet aftertaste. But the next day when everyone was around – out came the long rectangular aluminum pan! Nana had made another batch and she cut them in large squares, larger than usual and gave them out. I ate mine slowly, watching everyone else eat – and would catch Nana's eye and her twinkling silent inner laughter. She knew I'd learned my lesson. No words necessary this time. The wonder of food shared – what a comfort it could be – and that surprisingly you didn't even need all that much for it to fill you up, if the people you ate with were enjoying the company as much as the food.

I learned years later that the word 'company' comes from the Latin (and in many other languages it's the same) meaning 'those you break bread with'. I just learned it early through 'those you break brownies with!'

NANA'S RECIPE FOR BROWNIES (WITH WALNUTS)
*For 13x9 inch pan (they'll just be thicker in a smaller one)*
4 eggs
2 cups sugar
⅔ cup shortening
2 pinches of salt
4 squares of baking chocolate
1 cup of flour
2 teaspoons vanilla
2 cups of walnuts

Preheat oven to 325°. Beat eggs till foamy. Beat in salt. Add sugar gradually and continue beating. Melt chocolate and shortening together. Combine with egg and sugar mixture. Add flour gradually and beat well. Add vanilla. Add walnuts if desired. Spread in greased 13x9 inch baking pan. Bake at 325° for 30 minutes.

Test doneness by inserting straw (or toothpick) in centre – done if it comes out clean. Do not overbake, and let cool for at least forty-five minutes.

[67]

# — 17 —

# *Comfort Food – War Cake*

♣ ♦ ♥ ♠

I WAS BORN TOWARDS THE END OF WORLD WAR II. I have a picture of my dad on board ship, the USS Card, sailing from Samoa to Guam the morning I was born. My mom and aunts and my other sisters spent a lot of time with Nana during the war, though, of course, I don't remember much of it.

I vaguely remember a cake that Nana and my mom and aunts made. What intrigued me about is was that it was made in a coffee can so it was round, a rolled cake. It tasted more like a sweet bread than a cake – again I only realised that later when I ate actual cakes with sugar frosting. There wasn't any frosting on these cakes. We had them for birthdays and feast days, on Sundays for a treat and sometimes for what seemed to be no reason at all – or when we asked what the occasion was, the women around my mother, Nana and aunts would look at each other and smile and say, 'Well – Peg, or Jane, or Mary Elizabeth will be seeing your dad, or your uncle Bill or Jack when they're home on leave in San Diego or San Francisco in a couple of weeks'. Leave was short – only twenty-four or forty-eight hours and it was just adults, no children went. There was great excitement, anticipation, tears before and then after there were more tears and a different kind of feel, a kind of quiet or sadness or resignation that you could sense or fear that would creep back into the house again.

These memories and loose connections surfaced only lately – after September 11, 2001. People struggled to get home that day, walking bridges, tunnels, car-pooling, stunned, wept-out, shattered. And those who waited for them to come home had it just as hard. And I started hearing stories over the past four to five years of people getting home, crying, sobbing, falling into each others' arms and then sitting down to eat long after dark, after midnight or 3.00 am on September 12, 2001. And what they were served was war cake. It's a celebration food laced with memory and silent acknowledgement of the suffering, loss, and the reality that everything had shifted. Everything was more tenuous and less permanent and there-fore more precious. This was especially true on the northeast coast of the US where my family and so many dear friends lived and still live – in New York, New Jersey, Connecticut, Washington, DC, Maryland, Virginia, Massachusetts. They'd eat in silence, bites feeding body and soul, and sometimes feeding each other from the same piece, using the same fork. They shared cake, shared hope, shared memories, griefs, so much unspeakable, unwordable. It was not just about family or friends, but so many people one would think were strangers who suddenly were not.

The war cake, the comfort food declared our humanity in the face of violence, inhumanity, horror and irretrievable loss, abrupt endings, aborted lives. While people were telling me about baking war cake again on that day and in the days that followed, I found a poem from Guatamala, written by a man who had lived through the wars there and lost so many too. It resonated with why we go backwards in time looking for traditions that redeem us, reposition us in the world and feed us courage and hope in spite of all that transpires around us.

WALKING BACKWARD
Once in a while
I walk backward:
it's my way of
remembering.
if I only walked
forward,

[69]

I could tell you
how to forget.

– Humberto Ak'abal*

It is short. Sometimes what history does to us can only be integrated in short pieces, small bites, chewable so we can swallow them and not choke to death on them. We don't forget. We learn to mix it all in with memories, joys, hopes, searing grief, rage, silent retchings, singing, and we live. We live, perhaps, more truly, more gratefully and more hopefully, and more humanly than before, with others on this small planet. We do not let what has happened make us bitter but like the taste – even of war cake – in our mouths, minds and hearts – we can know compassion and be with all the others in the world. Still.

There are two recipes for war cake included here: one from New Jersey/New York and one from Canadian friends down east in Nova Scotia and the surrounding area. They shared the recipe and stories and feelings about 9/11, about WWII, about now and the possibility of a future where no one would ever eat war cake again. Tacked onto one of the many recipes I was given when I started telling about war cake and the kind of comfort both the cake and the words brought to people was a quote from Albert Camus: 'No government is ever pure or wise enough to claim the power to kill.' It was, somehow, part of the recipe of making the cake.

WAR CAKE
2 cups brown sugar
2 teaspoons cinnamon
2 tablespoons shortening
1 ½ teaspoons ground cloves

---

* A K'iche poet from Guatamala. In 'Poems I Brought Down from the Mountain', quoted in *Resistance, Repression, Refuge and Healing in Guatamala*, 2004, Power House Books.

2 cups of hot water
1 teaspoon ground ginger
1 package seedless raisins
2 level teaspoons salt
3 cups of flour sifted with 2 teaspoons baking soda

Put first eight ingredients in a saucepan. Simmer gently for 10 minutes. Watch the time carefully. When cooled, add the sifted flour and baking soda. Bake at 350° for 1 hour.

Enjoy.

[with thanks to Rose, downeast Canada]


WAR CAKE (NEW JERSEY/NEW YORK)
1 cup sugar
1 teaspoon cinnamon
2 cups water
½ teaspoon cloves
1 lb raisins
3 cups flour
2 tablespoons shortening
1 teaspoon baking soda
½ teaspoon baking powder

Put sugar, water, raisins, shortening, cinnamon and cloves in saucepan. Boil five minutes. Set aside to cool. Mix sifted flour, soda, salt and baking powder. Add to first mixture. Mix well. Pour into a greased pan. Bake in slow oven. 300°. 1–1 ½ hours.

[Thanks to Margaret Ann]

# Afterword

♣  ♦  ♥  ♠

FOR A LONG TIME I HAVE KNOWN THAT I WANT TO live like that shooting star she loved so, so that I will be standing at that gate, and welcoming in as many as I can and I suspect I have to be extra careful about anyone I would dub 'foe' or 'enemy' or one of 'them' here on earth. My nana shadows me, whispering out of the mist and the starry night that 'home is where they have to take you in' (quoting Robert Frost) and she's always saying, 'Sweetie, God never takes his eye off of you – he's watching you every minute, knows everything you do, everything about you – cause he loves you so much – just like your Nana does. Don't break his heart. Don't break my heart. So many folks are waiting on you. Find that one thing no one else will ever do – for God, or the earth, and do it in style, with grace and panache, and with everything you've got! Once you finally get it – that life is forever – than everything here is just practice for there!'

In the interim, until I see her again, may we, her grandchildren, and great grandchildren and all the people she managed to crowd into her heart, inaugurate those thousand years of peace. What my Nana knew in her wisdom and love and passed on to me and to all who hear her words. Thank you, Nana, thank you.

## A Word of Gratitude

Nana gave me so much – some through immediate contact with her and more through my father, her eldest son; my mother, through my aunt Jane, her eldest daughter (Jane died two days after her 95th birthday in 2004) and through presence – in photographs, objects she cherished, passed on, letters, words. Under all of it there is a foundation based on food. Food is meant to be eaten together, shared, given graciously, to friend and foe alike. No one is ever to be left to go hungry, eat alone regularly or live without what is necessary to survive and to really live – the food and bread of justice, hope, peace, possibilities for their children and grandchildren, sanctuary and shelter, daily dignity, care of body, mind and soul.

That is why, I guess, one of the quotations on her remembrance card at her funeral was from the gospel of John 10: 'I have come that you might have life, and have it ever more abundantly.' Those words, in a nutshell, a coffee can, a long rectangular brownie pan (or a pot of marrow bones, or a loaf of black bread) were the core, the heart of her life. This is her legacy that brings me comfort, that feeds me daily and makes me wish I had more time with her – as an adult, to be friends with her and exalt in her presence. And so I pray, that I will honour her memory in imitation, living my life ever more abundantly and bringing that life to others so that they may know wisdom, strength and delight – that they might catch that twinkle that was in her eye so often, peering out over her granny glasses, in me and in all the time I am given to share. This is the reason for this book of memories and gleanings passed on – along with the brownies and the war cake. Bon appétit to you all! My nana, I'm sure, would have loved having you all over, welcomed you into her house, for dinner, for a ballgame or for a poker game!

*Other Books by*
*Megan McKenna*

♣   ♦   ♥   ♠

# The Hour of the Tiger

♣ ◆ ♥ ♠

ISBN: 978 1 84730 079 9

The Hour of the Tiger: Facing Our Fears is about the present moment – every moment. It is about facing life and death, fear and love, about the hard issues of life and all the mysterious deep places of living too.

Tigers are an apt image for human beings who face their fears instead of becoming part of a herd that panics and runs, easily frightened by others who seek to manipulate fear for their own ends.

The tiger, on the verge of extinction, tells us that we must walk the edge, move to the margins and approach the gates of mystery so that we can live fully human lives.

All of life is a mystery and there are lots of edges and margins all reeking of the mystery of the unknown and the fullness of life yet to be known, experienced, embraced and lived.

— MEGAN McKENNA —

## Harm Not the Earth

♣  ♦  ♥  ♠

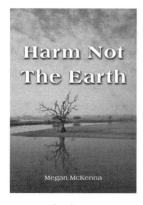

ISBN: 978 1 84730 024 9

Harm Not the Earth is a wake-up call which tells us that it is time to start bearing fruit, not for personal sanctification or salvation, but for the good of all. Megan McKenna tells us that if we are to be the followers of Jesus who is the fullness of life and sanctuary for all, who loved gardens and mountains and the sea and prayed that we might all be one in God as God is in us, then it is time for us to shift our attitudes towards who we think God is, what we think we are on this earth for and what it means to live and be responsible for creation 'in the image and likeness of God'.

# *Lent: Daily Readings*

♣ ♦ ♥ ♠

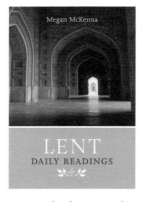

ISBN: 978 1 84730 104 8

Megan McKenna walks with us through the forty days of Lent and Holy Week. In two handy volumes – *Sunday Readings* and *Daily Readings* – stories and reflections are available for all three liturgical cycles, showing us how to imitate Jesus, encouraging us to resist temptation and to find our strengh in the Eurcharist, the Word of God and prayer throughout the Lenten season.

This book includes readings for each day of the week including Megan's reflections as well as a brief story that illuminates the text.

— MEGAN MCKENNA —

# *Lent: Sunday Readings*

♣ ♦ ♥ ♠

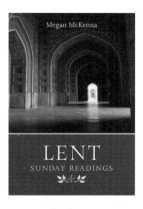

This book includes Sunday readings for Cycles A, B and C, including Palm Sunday and the Triduum. The three separate cycles of meditation for each Sunday include a unique story that illustrates and enriches the message of each reading, showing how it can empower us.

ISBN: 978 1 84730 099 7